WORD PRO

SHORTCUTS IN WORD 2000

ABOUT THIS BOOK

Shortcuts in Word 2000 is for people who already have some experience of Microsoft's Word 2000, and who want to speed up and customize their writing and formatting of documents.

WORD CONTAINS A WIDE VARIETY OF methods for customizing the program to reflect the way in which you work. Everyone uses Word differently, so this book will help you to build in your own preferences. These might include the look of the toolbars and screen, spelling preferences, or the many ways in which text that you use frequently can be made instantly available. There is also a comprehensive listing of those invaluable keyboard shortcuts that are useful to almost everyone.

The chapters and the subsections present this information using step-by-step sequences. Virtually every step is accompanied by an illustration showing how your screen should look at each stage.

The book assumes that you know how to enter text into documents; how to change or correct the text; how to choose where to save documents; and how then to find and open the documents.

The book contains several features to help you understand both what is happening and what you need to do. A labeled Word window is included to show you where to find the important elements in Word. This is followed by an illustration of the rows of buttons, or toolbars, at the top of the screen, to help you find your way around these controls.

Command keys, such as ENTER and CTRL, are shown in these rectangles: Enter↵ and Ctrl, so that there's no confusion, for example, over whether you should press that key, or type the letters "ctrl." Cross-references are shown in the text as left- or right-hand page icons: ◁ and ▷. The page number and the reference are shown at the foot of the page.

As well as the step-by-step sections, there are boxes that explain a feature in detail, and tip boxes that provide alternative methods and shortcuts. Finally, at the back, you will find a glossary explaining new terms and a comprehensive index.

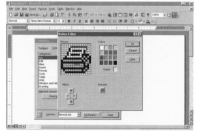

ESSENTIAL **DK** COMPUTERS

WORD PROCESSING

SHORTCUTS IN WORD 2000

SUE ETHERINGTON

LONDON, NEW YORK, MUNICH, MELBOURNE, DELHI

SENIOR EDITOR Jacky Jackson
SENIOR ART EDITOR Sarah Cowley
DTP DESIGNER Julian Dams and Rajen Shah
PRODUCTION CONTROLLER Melanie Dowland

MANAGING EDITOR Adèle Hayward
MANAGING ART EDITOR Karen Self
CATEGORY PUBLISHER Stephanie Jackson

Produced for Dorling Kindersley Limited by
Design Revolution Limited, Queens Park Villa,
30 West Drive, Brighton, East Sussex BN2 0QW
EDITORIAL DIRECTOR Ian Whitelaw
SENIOR DESIGNER Andrew Easton
PROJECT EDITOR John Watson
DESIGNER Paul Bowler

First published in Great Britain in 2000 by
Dorling Kindersley Limited,
80 Strand, London WC2R 0RL

Revised edition 2002
A Penguin publication

2 4 6 8 10 9 7 5 3 1

A CIP catalogue record for this book is available from the British Library.

ISBN 0-7513-4635-7

Colour reproduced by Colourscan, Singapore
Printed and bound in Italy by Graphicom

For our complete catalogue visit
www.dk.com

CONTENTS

MICROSOFT WORD

Microsoft Word has been around for well over a decade and, with each new release, continues to add to its reputation as the world's leading word-processing program.

WHAT CAN WORD DO?

The features contained in Word make it one of the most flexible word-processing programs available. Word can be used to write anything from shopping lists to large publications that contain, in addition to the main text, illustrations and graphics, charts, tables and graphs, captions, headers and footers, cross-references, footnotes, indexes, and glossaries – all of which are easily managed by Word.

Word can check spelling and grammar, check text readability, search and replace text, import data, sort data, perform calculations, and provide templates for many types of documents from memos to web pages. The comprehensive and versatile design, formatting, and layout options in Word make it ideal for desktop publishing on almost any scale. In short, there's very little that Word cannot do.

WHAT IS A WORD DOCUMENT?

In its simplest form, a Word document is a sequence of characters that exists in a computer's memory. Using Word, a document can be edited, added to, and given a variety of layouts. Once the document has been created, there are a large number of actions that can be carried out, such as saving, printing, or sending the document as an email.

LAUNCHING WORD

Word launches just like any other program running in Windows. With the Windows desktop on screen, you can launch Word as the only program running, or you can run Word alongside other software to exchange data with other applications.

1 LAUNCHING BY THE START MENU

● Place the mouse cursor over the **Start** button on the Taskbar and click with the left mouse button.
● Move the cursor up the pop-up menu until **Programs** is highlighted. A submenu of programs appears to the right.
● Move the cursor down the menu to **Microsoft Word** and left-click again. (If Microsoft Word is missing from the Programs menu, it may be under **Microsoft Office**.)
● The Microsoft Word window opens ⬚.

2 LAUNCHING BY A SHORTCUT

● You may already have a Word icon on screen, which is a shortcut to launching Word. If so, double-click on the icon.
● The Microsoft Word window opens ⬚.

 The Word Window 8

THE WORD WINDOW

At first, Word's document window may look like a space shuttle computer display. However, you'll soon discover that similar commands and actions are neatly grouped together. This "like-with-like" layout helps you quickly understand where you should be looking on the window for what you want. Click and play while you read this.

THE WORD WINDOW

1 Title bar
2 Menu bar
Contains the main menus.
3 Standard toolbar
Buttons for frequent actions.
4 Formatting toolbar
Main layout options.
5 Tab selector
Clicking selects type of tab.
6 Left-indent buttons
Used to set left indents.
7 Ruler
Displays margins and tabs.
8 Right-indent button
Used to set right indent.
9 Insertion point
Shows where typing appears.
10 Text area
Area for document text.
11 Split box
Creates two text panes.
12 Scroll-up arrow
Moves up the document.
13 Scroll-bar box
Moves text up or down.
14 Vertical scroll bar
Used to move through text.

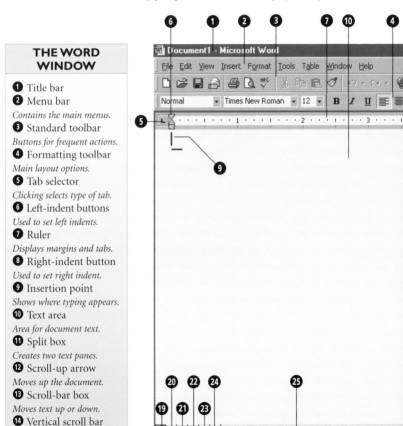

TOOLBAR LAYOUT

If Word doesn't show the Formatting toolbar below the Standard toolbar, first place the cursor over the Formatting toolbar "handle." When the four-headed arrow appears, (right), hold down the mouse button and "drag" the toolbar into position.

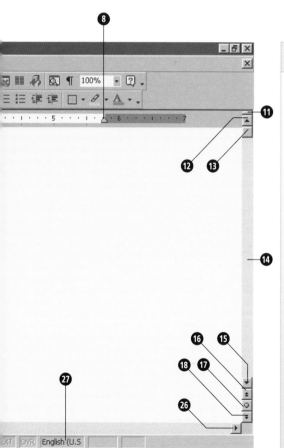

THE WORD WINDOW

⑮ Scroll-down arrow
Moves down the document.

⑯ Page-up button
Shows previous page of text.

⑰ Select browse object
Opens browse options menu.

⑱ Page-down button
Displays next page of text.

⑲ Normal view
Default document view.

⑳ Web layout view
Web-browser page view.

㉑ Page layout view
Printed-page view of text.

㉒ Outline view
Shows document's structure.

㉓ Left-scroll arrow
Shows the text to the left.

㉔ Scroll-bar box
Moves text horizontally.

㉕ Horizontal scroll bar
To view wide documents.

㉖ Right-scroll arrow
Shows the text to the right.

㉗ Language
Spelling, thesaurus, and proofing settings.

THE WORD TOOLBARS

Word provides a range of toolbars where numerous commands and actions are available. The principal toolbars are the Standard toolbar and the Formatting toolbar, which contain the most frequently used features of Word. There are also more than 20 other toolbars available for display. Click on **Tools** in the Menu bar, move the cursor down to **Customize,** and click the mouse button. The **Customize** dialog box opens. Click the **Toolbars** tab to view the variety of toolbars available.

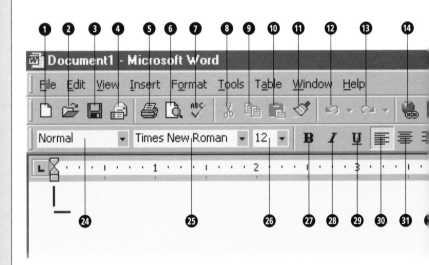

THE STANDARD TOOLBAR

1 New document
2 Open folder or file
3 Save
4 Email
5 Print
6 Print preview
7 Spelling and grammar
8 Cut
9 Copy text
10 Paste text
11 Format painter
12 Undo action(s)
13 Redo action(s)
14 Insert hyperlink
15 Tables and borders
16 Insert table
17 Insert Excel worksheet
18 Columns
19 Drawing toolbar
20 Document map
21 Show/hide formatting marks
22 Zoom view of text
23 Microsoft Word help

CUSTOMIZING A TOOLBAR

To add a Close button to a toolbar, click on **Tools** in the Menu bar and select **Customize**. Click on the **Commands** tab of the **Customize** dialog box. Scroll down the Commands menu to display the **Close** button. Place the cursor over the button, hold down the mouse button, drag the icon to the toolbar, and release the mouse button.

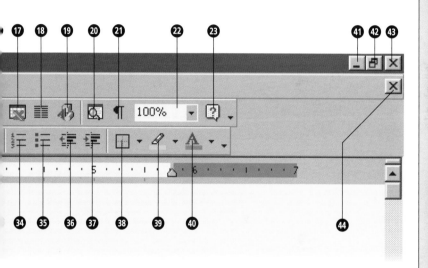

THE FORMATTING TOOLBAR

- ㉔ Style selector
- ㉕ Font selector
- ㉖ Font size selector
- ㉗ Bold
- ㉘ Italic
- ㉙ Underline
- ㉚ Left-aligned text
- ㉛ Centered text
- ㉜ Right-aligned text
- ㉝ Justified text
- ㉞ Numbered list
- ㉟ Bulleted list
- ㊱ Decrease indent
- ㊲ Increase indent
- ㊳ Outside border
- ㊴ Highlight color
- ㊵ Font color
- ㊶ Minimize Word
- ㊷ Maximize/Restore
- ㊸ Close Word
- ㊹ Close document

CUSTOMIZING TOOLBARS

Besides the default Standard and Formatting toolbars, Word offers many other useful toolbars. You can also create your own custom toolbar containing just the buttons you need.

SHOWING, MOVING, AND HIDING TOOLBARS

There is a range of available toolbars from which you can choose to view those that are most useful to the tasks that you are performing in Word. Making a toolbar visible is extremely simple, and you can then choose to place it in the most convenient position on the screen. When you have finished with a toolbar, it can again be hidden. In the example shown here, we will use the WordArt toolbar.

1 SHOWING TOOLBARS

● Position the mouse arrow anywhere on the Menu bar, the Standard toolbar, or the Formatting toolbar at the top of the Word window ⌐.
● Click on the right mouse button (right-click) and a list of all the available toolbars is displayed in a drop-down menu.
● You will see that the two default toolbars – Standard and Formatting – that are already shown on the screen are checked.

The Word Window
8

● To bring up the WordArt toolbar, drag the mouse arrow down the list until **WordArt** is highlighted.

● Now click on the left mouse button, and the WordArt toolbar appears on the screen.

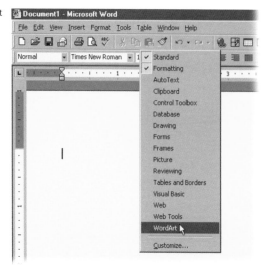

● When a toolbar is shown onscreen, it may appear as a "floating" toolbar in the screen area, away from the edges, or as a "docked" toolbar, attached to an edge of the screen in the same way as the Standard and Formatting toolbars. In either case you can move it to your preferred position.

Floating toolbar

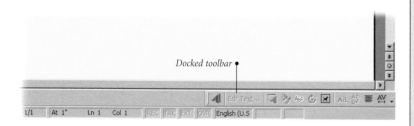

Docked toolbar

2 MOVING DOCKED TOOLBARS

● To move a docked toolbar to the top of the screen to join the Standard and Formatting toolbars, start by positioning the mouse arrow over the extreme left side of the toolbar, where you can see a vertical gray line.
● The arrow turns into a four-headed black arrow.
● Now click the left mouse button and hold it down.

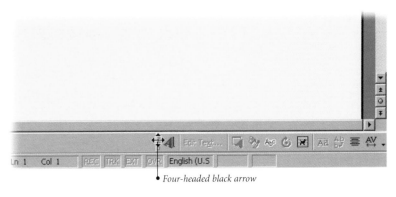

● Four-headed black arrow

● Drag the mouse upward and the docked WordArt toolbar changes into a floating toolbar 🗋.
● Drag the toolbar further up the screen until it is over any part of the Formatting toolbar 🗋.
● When it changes shape again and slots in at the top of the screen, release the mouse button.

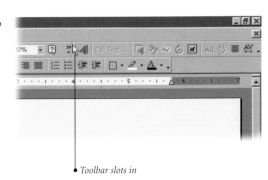

● Toolbar slots in

🗋 **13 Showing toolbars**

🗋 **11 Formatting toolbar**

3 MOVING FLOATING TOOLBARS

● Click on the blue bar at the top of the toolbar next to the word **WordArt**, and then drag the toolbar over part of the Formatting toolbar at the top of the screen. When the WordArt toolbar changes shape again and slots in at the top of the screen, release the mouse button.

4 HIDING DOCKED TOOLBARS

To hide any docked toolbar, the operation is the reverse of making a toolbar visible.

● Position the mouse arrow anywhere on the menu or toolbars at the top of the screen, as before ⌐|.

● Right click the mouse button, and the list of all of the available toolbars is displayed.

● Click the **WordArt** entry to deselect it, and the WordArt toolbar disappears from the screen.

Instant hiding
To hide any floating toolbar quickly, just click on the X at the top right of the toolbar.

ADDING AND REMOVING BUTTONS

There is a wide range of commonly used toolbar buttons available in Word that are not shown as standard. These can be found via the toolbars themselves, providing an easy way to customize your toolbars to suit the way you work.

1 VIEWING THE CHOICE

● Click on the down arrow at the right-hand end of the Standard toolbar. The **Add or Remove Buttons** panel appears.

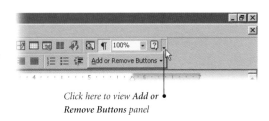

*Click here to view **Add or Remove Buttons** panel*

● Hold the mouse over the **Add or Remove Buttons** button (or click on it) and the drop down list of available buttons appears. Using this list, you can decide which buttons you wish to appear on your Standard toolbar, and which you may wish to remove.

● As well as the **Print** icon on your toolbar, you will see that there is a second **Print** icon at the bottom of the list, under Microsoft Word Help. This one displays the **Print** dialog box, saving you clicking on **File** and then **Print** each time you need to set up some print options. As an example, we are going to add this button to the Standard toolbar.

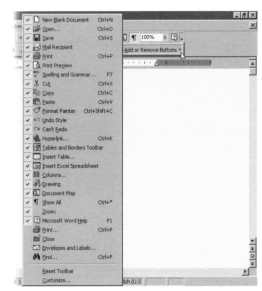

2 ADDING THE BUTTON

● To add the second Print option to the Standard toolbar, click on the icon.

● A checkmark appears in the checkbox next to the icon. Now click anywhere on the screen to close the list of buttons.

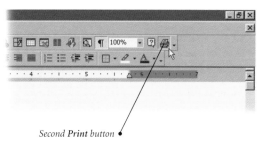

✓ 🔲 Tables and Borders Toolbar
✓ ▦ Insert Table...
✓ 🔲 Insert Excel Spreadsheet
✓ ▤ Columns...
✓ ✏ Drawing
✓ 🔲 Document Map
✓ ¶ Show All   Ctrl+*
✓ 🔲 Zoom:
✓ ? Microsoft Word Help   F1
  🖨 Print...   Ctrl+P
  📁 Close
  ✉ Envelopes and Labels...
  🔍 Find...   Ctrl+F

  Reset Toolbar
Ln 1 Customize...   lish (U.S

● The new **Print** icon now appears at the right-hand end of the toolbar.

● To test the button, click on the new **Print** button and the **Print** dialog box will appear.

🔛 🔲 🖼 ▤ ✏ 🔲 ¶ 100% ▾ 🔲 🖨 ▾
≡ ≡ ≡ ⋮≡ ⋮≡ 🔲 ▾ 🔳 ▾ 🗚 ▾
· · · 4 · · · ¡ · · · 5 · · · ¡ · · · △ · 6 · ¡ · · · △ · · · ¡ · · 7

*Second **Print** button* ●

● Click on **Cancel** at the bottom of the **Print** dialog box to close it.

Restore to Default

If you want to restore the toolbars to their default settings, open the list of available buttons as described above and click on **Reset Toolbar** at the bottom of the list.

Print   ? ✕
Printer
Name: 🖨 HP DeskJet 400 Printer   ▾   Properties
Status: Idle
Type: HP DeskJet 400 Printer
Where: LPT1:   ☐ Print to file
Comment:

Page range   Copies
● All   Number of copies: 1 ⬍
○ Current page ○ Selection
○ Pages: [icons] ☑ Collate
Enter page numbers and/or page ranges
separated by commas. For example, 1,3,5–12

                               Zoom
Print what: Document   ▾   Pages per sheet: 1 page   ▾
Print: All pages in range ▾ Scale to paper size: No Scaling ▾

Options...   OK   Cancel

3 EDITING THE BUTTON IMAGE

● To distinguish between the new **Print** button and the original (which prints a single copy of the current document), we are going to color the new one blue.

● Click on **Tools** in the menu bar, and choose **Customize** from the drop-down menu.

● Leaving the **Customize** dialog box open, right-click the new **Print** icon on the toolbar. Another drop-down menu appears.

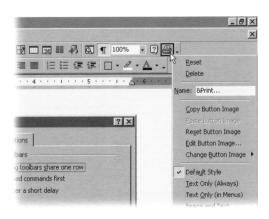

● Click on **Edit Button Image** and the **Button Editor** dialog box will be displayed.

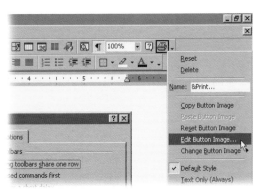

Unchangeable icons
Although you can edit the image of a **File** menu button, you cannot change it to a different icon.

● The **Button Editor** dialog box displays the existing **Print** icon image, in a pixelated form, as well as a color palette.

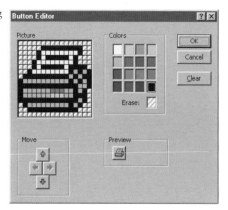

● Click on the blue block in the palette (to select the color that you want to use).

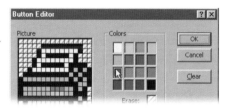

● When the **Print** icon in the **Picture** box is as you want it, click on **OK**.

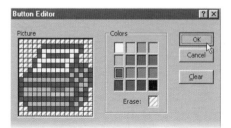

● The **Print** icon on the toolbar is now blue.

● Click on **Close** in the **Customize** dialog box.

● We now have two printer icons. One will just print out a single copy of a document, and the other will automatically display the **Print** dialog box.

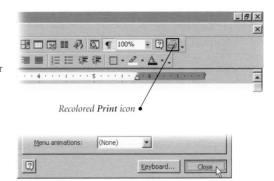

Recolored Print icon ●

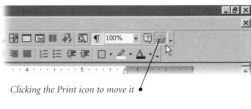

4 REPOSITIONING THE BUTTON

● The two **Print** icons should be next to each other, so we are going to move the new one.

● Holding down the [Alt] key on the keyboard (to the left of the spacebar), click on the **Print** icon to be moved and hold down the mouse button.

Clicking the Print icon to move it ●

● Now drag the blue **Print** button, in the form of a small rectangular block, to its new location and release the mouse button.

● The two printer icons are now next to each other.

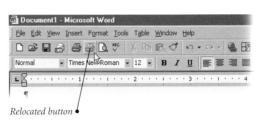

Relocated button ●

5 CHANGING BUTTON STYLE

If, for example, you confuse the icon for **Format Painter** (the paintbrush) with the **Paste** button next to it, you can change the **Format Painter** icon to a picture of your choice.

● Click on **Tools** in the menu bar, and choose **Customize** from the drop-down menu.

● Leaving the **Customize** dialog box open, right-click the **Format Painter** icon on the Standard toolbar and another drop-down menu is displayed, with **Format Painter** displayed in the **Name:** panel.

● Select **Change Button Image** and a panel of different icons is displayed. We are going to choose the icon that shows two identical pages – showing that one page has the same format as the other.

Copying a Button

To copy a toolbar button, follow the steps to move a button, but hold down the [Ctrl] and [Alt] keyboard keys, simultaneously.

● Click on the new icon, and this will now be displayed as the **Format Painter** button on the Standard toolbar. Click on **Close** in the **Customize** dialog box.

6 DELETING BUTTONS

● To delete a button from a toolbar, click on **Tools** in the menu bar and choose **Customize** from the drop-down menu.

● Now right-click on the toolbar button to be deleted (in this case the Format Painter icon that we have just changed). Another drop-down menu appears.

● Click on **Delete** in the drop-down menu, and the button is deleted from the toolbar.

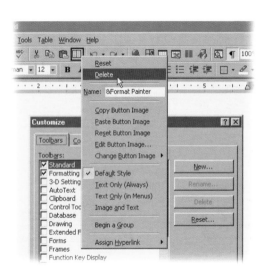

The button is deleted ●

CREATING NEW BUTTONS

Using the **Customize** option in the **Tools** menu, it is also possible to add useful buttons to the existing toolbars, add icons to the buttons, remove a button from a toolbar, or change the button's appearance and create your own personalized toolbar.

1 ADDING A NEW BUTTON

In this example, we are going to add a button to the Standard toolbar to take us directly to the **Save As** window, rather than having to use **File** in the menu bar.

● Click on the **Tools** menu, then on **Customize**.

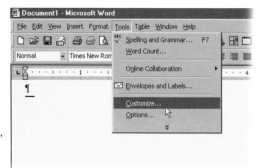

● The **Customize** dialog box is displayed.
● Click on the **Commands** tab at the top of the box to bring it to the front.

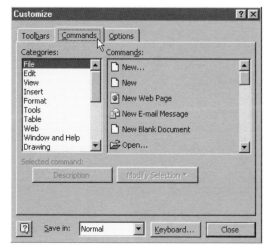

● The Category we are interested in is **File**, since the **Save As** option is found in the **File** drop-down menu, so click on **File** in the **Categories:** list, if it is not already highlighted.

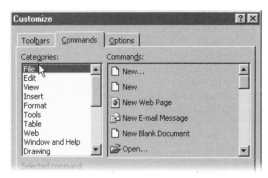

● Scroll down the **Commands:** panel to the right of the **Categories:** list and highlight **Save As....**
● Click on **Save As...** and drag it to the place in the Standard toolbar where you wish the new button to be.
● Release the mouse button, and the words **Save As** now appear on the Standard toolbar.

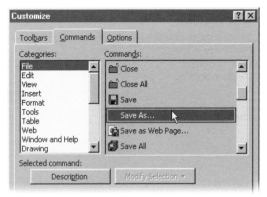

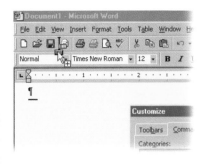

● *The Save As... button now appears on the toolbar*

2 ADDING A BUTTON ICON

Although we have **Save As...** on the toolbar, it would be better if it also had an icon as well, so let's add an appropriate icon to the text.

● Leaving the **Customized** box open on the screen, right-click the **Save As** text on the toolbar.

● From the drop-down menu, hold the mouse arrow over **Change Button Image**.

● On the drop-down menu, click on an icon that you feel is appropriate for **Save As**. In our example, we have chosen the "Arrow into disk" icon.

● This icon now appears as a button on the toolbar next to the **Save As...** text.

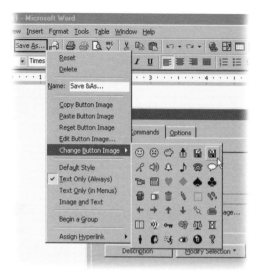

● *Newly created Save As button*

● Click on **Close** on the **Customize** window.

● To test the new button, simply click on it and check that the **Save As** window appears, and click on **Cancel** at the bottom of the screen to close the window.

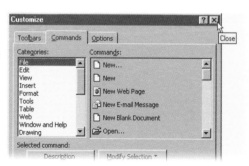

CREATING YOUR OWN CUSTOM TOOLBAR

You might wish to create a toolbar that reflects the kind of work that you do and the tasks that you use within Word 2000 on a regular basis. This can save a great deal of time and effort, and it is easy to set up your own customized toolbar.

1 OPENING A NEW TOOLBAR

● Click on **Tools** in the menu bar, and choose **Customize** from the drop-down menu.

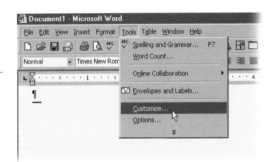

● Click on the **Toolbars** tab at the top of the **Customize** dialog box to bring it to the front.

● Click on the **New** button at the top of the right-hand side of the window and the **New Toolbar** dialog box is displayed.

● The **Toolbar name:** field is highlighted. This is where you should enter the name of your new toolbar. In our example we are going to call it **Daily Working**.

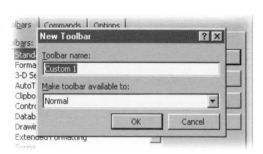

● Leave the text in the **Make toolbar available to:** field as **Normal**. This means that the toolbar will be available to you from now on whenever you open a new document based on the normal template.

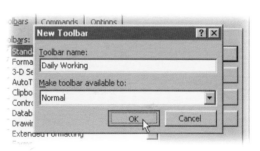

● Click on **OK** at the bottom of the window, and a small "floating" toolbar appears on the screen.

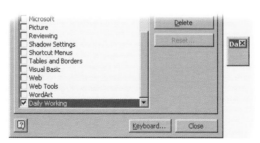

2 ADDING BUTTONS TO THE TOOLBAR

● Now that we have our new toolbar, we need to select the commands that we wish to have on it. We will start by adding the **Undo** button to the new toolbar.

● In the **Customize** dialog box, click on the **Commands** tab to bring it to the front.

● Under the **Categories:** list, click on **Edit**, and then select the command **Undo** from the **Commands:** list.

● Holding down the mouse button, drag and drop the **Undo** button onto the new toolbar.

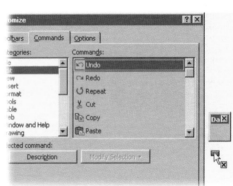

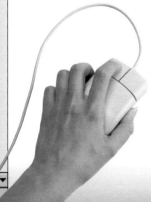

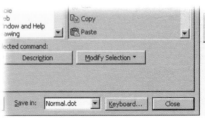

● To add further command buttons to the new toolbar, repeat these steps for the **Redo**, **Repeat**, **Clear**, and **Select All** commands, all of which are to be found in the **Edit** category.

● Click on **Close** at the bottom of the **Customize** window and the newly created toolbar is complete.

● This customized floating toolbar can be "docked" at the top of the screen like any other toolbar .

DELETING YOUR OWN TOOLBAR

To delete a custom toolbar, click on **Tools** in the Menu bar, select **Customize** from the drop-down menu, and click on the **Toolbar** tab to bring it to the front of the **Customize** dialog box. Click on the toolbar you wish to delete and then click **Delete**. The toolbar is deleted.

It is not possible to delete a built-in toolbar.

15 **Moving floating toolbars**

CUSTOMIZING WORD

There are three text correction features that you can customize to suit your needs. The spell checker, AutoText, and AutoCorrect can all be tailored to handle your own unique words and text.

WORD'S SPELLING OPTIONS

Word recognizes that people want their documents checked in different ways, and that many documents will contain unique spellings that, although unrecognized by Word, are nonetheless correct. Here you will learn how to control Word's spell checking, and how to tell Word that your own, unrecognized, spellings are correct.

1 CONTROLLING THE SPELL CHECK

● The principal tools for controlling how Word spell checks a document are contained in the **Spelling & Grammar** tab of the **Options** dialog box.
● To open this tab, begin by clicking on **Options** in the **Tools** menu.

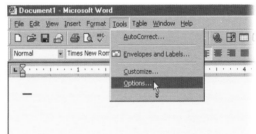

SKIP TEXT IN A SPELL CHECK

If there is a section of text that you don't want Word to check, begin by highlighting that piece of text. Select **Language** from the **Tools** menu and click on **Set Language.** In the dialog box, make sure there is a check mark in the **Do not check spelling or grammar** check box. That text will be ignored.

● The **Options** dialog box opens. Click on the **Spelling & Grammar** tab.

● The various ways in which you can control the way that Word checks your documents are shown in the annotated **Options** dialog box shown below.

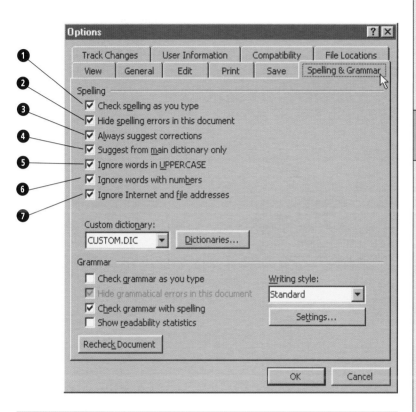

SPELLING OPTIONS

❶ With this box checked, Word places a wavy line beneath unknown words.
❷ Spelling errors, in this file only, will be hidden.
❸ Spelling suggestions are omitted in a spell check.
❹ Custom dictionary entries are ignored.
❺ This prevents unknown acronyms being checked.
❻ Codes, such as model numbers, are ignored.
❼ Word recognizes a Web address and can ignore it.

2 CUSTOMIZING A DICTIONARY

● The principal way to tell Word that the spelling of a unique word is correct is to add it to a Custom dictionary. Once you have done so, Word will no longer query this word.

● There are two ways to add a word to your Custom dictionary: first, when Word queries the spelling; and second, when you carry out a spell check.

WHEN WORD QUERIES A SPELLING

● If you have Word set up to check the spelling as you type, a red wavy line appears below any word that Word does not know.

● Place the insertion point over the queried word and right-click with the mouse button. A pop-up panel appears.

● Click on **Add** to add the word to your Custom dictionary.

● The red wavy line disappears and the word will not be queried again.

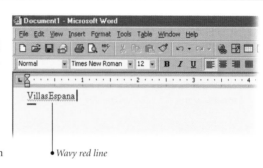

• Wavy red line

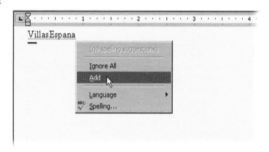

WHEN CARRYING OUT A SPELL CHECK

● This time the word **VillasItalia** has been typed in, and it is queried during a spell check. The **Spelling & Grammar** dialog box contains an **Add** button. Click on the **Add** button and the word is added to the Custom dictionary.

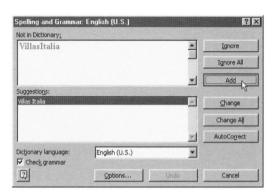

3 EDITING THE DICTIONARY

● You may have added a misspelled word to your dictionary in error, or you may wish to delete a word. These can be corrected easily. Begin by opening the **Spelling & Grammar** tab ⌐. Click on the **Dictionaries...** button.

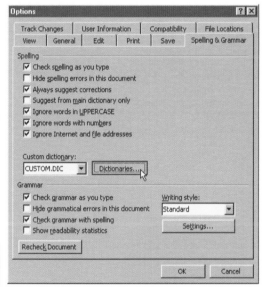

Correct language?
If you find that the **Add** option is grayed out, click on **Language** on the pop-up panel and make sure the correct language is selected.

30 Controlling the spell check

● The **Custom Dictionaries** dialog box opens. Make sure that the dictionary checkbox **CUSTOM.DIC** is checked. Click on **Edit** at the foot of the dialog box.

● Word displays an alert panel telling you that automatic spell checking stops when you edit a dictionary, and what to do. Click on **OK**.

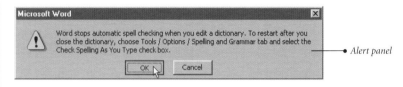

Word stops automatic spell checking when you edit a dictionary. To restart after you close the dictionary, choose Tools / Options / Spelling and Grammar tab and select the Check Spelling As You Type check box.

● Alert panel

● The contents of the Custom dictionary are listed on the screen as a Word document, named **CUSTOM.DIC**, which can be edited.

DELETING WORDS

If you wish to delete words from your dictionary, follow the steps shown here for editing, and delete the word as you would in any Word document.

● Let's assume that we should have left a space between **Villas** and **Italia**. Insert the space and click on the **Save** button on the Standard toolbar.

● Close the document and you are returned to your original document. Remember to open the **Spelling & Grammar** window and click on the **Check spelling as you type** checkbox before continuing with your document.

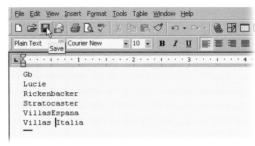

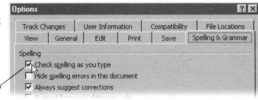

After editing the dictionary,
turn on the spell check again

USING AUTOTEXT

AutoText is a very useful feature in Word that stores your own text and graphics. These can then be inserted into your documents whenever they are required.

Each AutoText entry has a unique name, chosen by you, and when this is keyed in AutoText automatically inserts the text or graphics you have linked to the name.

1 CREATING AN AUTOTEXT ENTRY

● Let's assume that you wish to hold your business address in AutoText. Enter the address and set it as right-aligned text.

Align right button

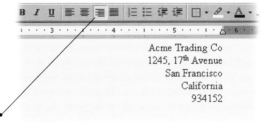

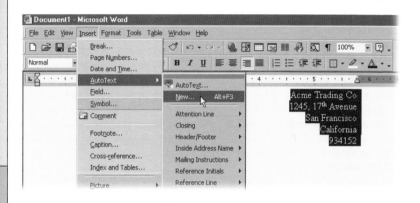

● Highlight the complete address, click on **Insert** on the Menu bar, followed by **AutoText,** and then **New**.
● The **Create AutoText** dialog box opens.
● Word suggests a name for the AutoText, but it can be made shorter so that there is less to enter. However, the name must be at least four characters long and any AutoText entry itself must be at least five characters. Edit the name to **Acme** as the AutoText name and click on **OK**.

AUTOTEXT ALTERNATIVE

Once you have set up an AutoText entry, you can also insert it into your document by clicking on **Insert**, then **AutoText**, and then on **Normal**. A submenu of all AutoText entries is displayed. Click on the one you require and its associated text or graphic is inserted into your document.

No to AutoText
If you do not want to insert the AutoText entry, simply continue typing and it disappears.

2 INSERTING AN AUTOTEXT ENTRY

● Open a new document and type **Acme**. The AutoText containing the first part of the address is displayed above the name.

● Press the [Enter ←] key and the address is inserted into the document exactly where you want it to be placed on the page.

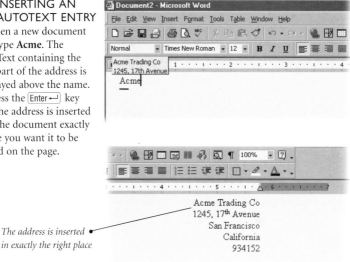

The address is inserted in exactly the right place

USING AUTOCORRECT

The AutoCorrect feature allows you to set up the automatic correction of words that you often misspell or mistype. Many common errors are already set up in

AutoCorrect, but you can easily add your own. You can also use it to capitalize words, such as days of the week, and to insert symbols such as © by entering (c).

1 AUTOCORRECT: ADDING WORDS

● As an example, we'll use the common misspelling: **decieve** for **deceive**.

● Click on **Tools** on the Menu bar and then on **AutoCorrect...** .

● The **AutoCorrect** dialog box opens. Click on the **AutoCorrect** tab to bring it to the front. In the **Replace:** text box, enter the incorrect spelling: **decieve**. In the **With:** text box, enter the correct spelling: **deceive**. Then click on **Add**.

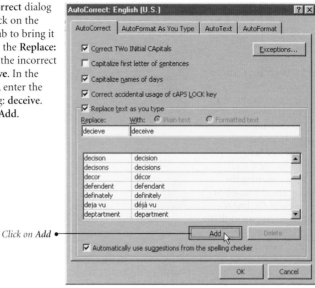

Click on Add ●

● The AutoCorrect entry that you have just made is now displayed in the list of AutoCorrect entries. Click on **Close** and each time that you now type **decieve**, it will be replaced automatically with the correct spelling.

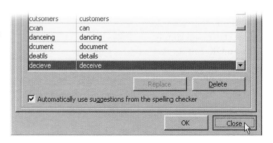

RESETTING AUTOCORRECT

If you wish to reset AutoCorrect so that entering (c) will always change to © again, use the steps outlined above to add a new entry to the list – in the **Replace:** box enter (c) and in the **With:** box type [Ctrl] + [Alt] + **C** to insert the symbol ©.

2 AUTOCORRECT: DELETING ITEMS

● There may be an AutoCorrect entry set up either by you or Word that is no longer required. For example, if you are listing points in a document as: (a) (b) (c), you do not want Word to change (c) to the symbol ©, which is already included in AutoCorrect.

● To remove this entry, begin by opening the **AutoCorrect** dialog box □.

● Click on the line of AutoCorrect entries that contains (c) to be replaced by ©, and click on **Delete**.

● In the **Replace:** text box, (c) appears, and in the **With:** text box, © appears. If you were to click on **Add** at this point, the AutoCorrect entry would be reinstated, but simply click on **OK**. Now when you type (c) in a document, it will not automatically change to ©.

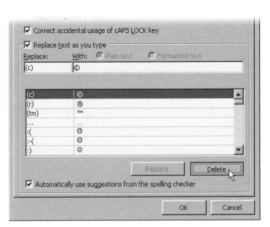

CUSTOMIZING AUTOCORRECT

In the **AutoCorrect** dialog box there are check boxes that you can use to set up AutoCorrect to correct errors such as a sequence of two initial capital letters or beginning a sentence with a lower-case letter. As these corrections are controlled by check boxes, you can disable them if required.

37 **AutoCorrect: Adding Words**

USING TEMPLATES

A template is a document that Word uses to base other documents on. It contains settings that include the font, font size, page layout, and any special formatting features and text.

CUSTOMIZING THE NORMAL TEMPLATE

By default, all new documents are based on the settings in the Normal template unless you specifically open a new document by using an alternative template. If there are settings in the Normal template that you have to change each time you open a new document, you can change these settings in the Normal template itself, and you will not have to reset them again.

1 CHANGING FONT AND INDENT

● The default font in the Normal template is Times New Roman, but perhaps you prefer to use Arial. In addition, you may need a wider left indent.

● The first step is to locate the Normal template. Click on **Tools** on the Menu bar, followed by **Options**, and then click on the **File Locations** tab in the **Options** dialog box.

● Click on **User templates** and click on **Modify...** .

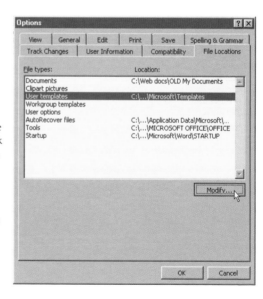

● The **Modify Location** dialog box opens. The location of the folder containing the User Templates is shown in the **Folder name:** text box. In the example, the full path is **C:\WINDOWS\ Application Data\ Microsoft\Templates**. Make a note of this path as you will need it to access the **Normal** template.
● Click on **OK** in this dialog box and click on **Close** at the foot of the **Options** dialog box.

● As you cannot amend a file while it is in use, the current document window must be closed, so click on **Close** in the **File** menu.

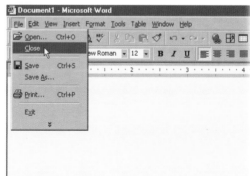

FILE EXTENSIONS

All files that are templates have a file extension of **.dot** (e.g. **Normal.dot**). Ordinary documents have an extension of **.doc**.

OPENING THE NORMAL TEMPLATE

● Click on **Open** button on the Standard toolbar.

● The **Open** dialog box appears. To find the **Normal** template, double-click on the following sequence of folders: **C:;** **Windows; Application Data; Microsoft;** and finally the **Templates** folder where the **Normal** template file is located.

● Click on **Normal** and click on **Open**.

● The template file, **Normal**, opens and can be edited as any other Word document. Begin to make the changes by clicking on the down arrow next to the Font selection box and select the font **Arial**.

UPDATING FILES

When a template is edited, existing documents based on that template are not affected. If you want an existing file to adopt the new settings, click on **Templates and Add-Ins** in the **Tools** menu and click in the **Automatically update document styles** check box before you open the document.

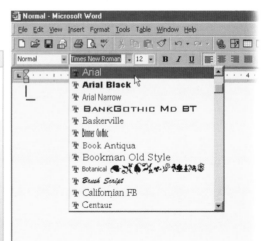

● Place the cursor over the lower rectangle at the left of the ruler until the **Left Indent** ScreenTip appears.

● Hold down the mouse button and drag the left indent to the half-inch position on the ruler.
● Release the mouse button and the new, wider indent is set.

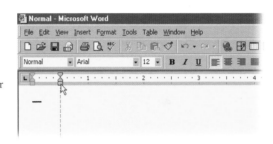

● Now click on **Save** in the **File** menu.
● The edited template cannot be used until you close Word and relaunch it. Close Word by clicking on **Exit** in the **File** menu.

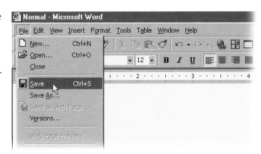

● Relaunch Word, and **Document1** appears onscreen as usual, but the font is now Arial and the left indent appears at the half-inch position. Each time you launch Word, the initial document will have these settings.

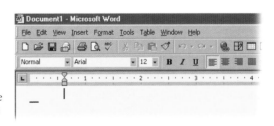

CREATING A NEW TEMPLATE

Templates can be created to contain any text and graphics that you require. These can include, for example, your business logo, your name and address, and any text that you need to be included in a series of documents. Once you have created the template, each document that you base on it will contain all those elements.

1 A TEMPLATE FROM A DOCUMENT

The easiest way to create a new template is to set up a document with the required formatting and save it as a template. We will set up a template for an agenda, with a logo, title, heading, and a date.

● Open a document based on the new **Normal** template and click on **Insert** on the Menu bar and select **Symbol...**.

● In the **symbol** dialog box, click on the down arrow next to the **Subset:** box and choose **Letterlike Symbols**.

Other symbols

You can view the symbols that are available in other fonts by clicking on the down arrow next to the **Font** selection box and clicking on a font in the drop-down menu.

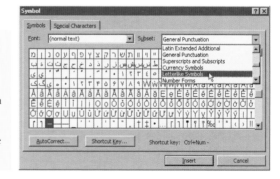

● Click on the Ω (omega) character and then on **Insert** at the foot of the dialog box. Then click on **Close** at the foot of the **Symbol** dialog box.

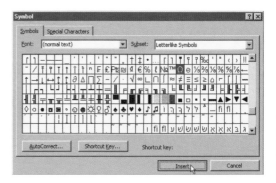

● Press [Enter ←] twice to create two line spaces below the Ω character and then enter: **Dallas Baseball Club**.

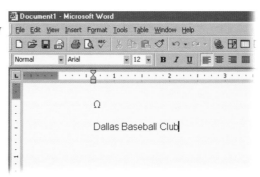

● Leave another two lines and enter: **AGENDA**.

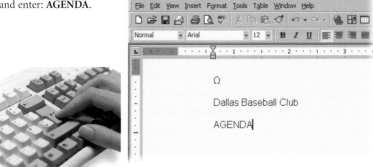

● Highlight all three lines and:
(1) Click on the **Bold** button.
(2) Click on the **Underline** button.
(3) Click on the **Center** button.
(4) Make the font size **14**.

● Place the insertion point at the end of AGENDA and press Enter↵.

● Click the **Align Left** button and deselect the **Underline** setting by clicking the button again. Leave two more lines spaces and enter **Attendees**.

● Use the Tab⇆ key to move to the 4-inch ruler position and type **Date** followed by a space.

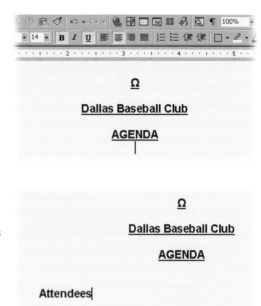

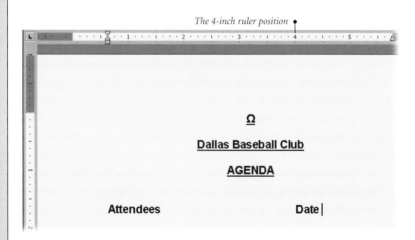

The 4-inch ruler position ●

● Click on **Insert** on the Menu bar and then choose **Date and Time...** .

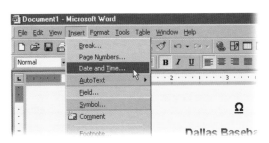

● The **Date and Time** dialog box opens. In our example, we have chosen the format: **29-Sep-00**. Click on **OK**.

● Now the agenda can be saved as a template, which can be used as the basis for all club agendas in the future. Click on **File** on the Menu bar and then click on **Save As**.

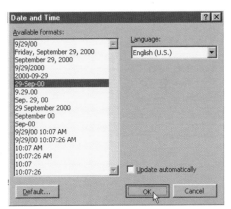

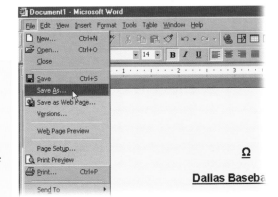

Updated date
If you click in the **Update automatically** check box in the **Date and Time** dialog box, then each time you open the document, the date will show the current date.

● The **Save As** dialog box
opens. If the **Templates**
folder is not shown in the
Save in: text box, navigate
to it as we did earlier ⌐.
You can see in the **File
name:** box that Word has
suggested the file name:
Dallas Baseball Club.

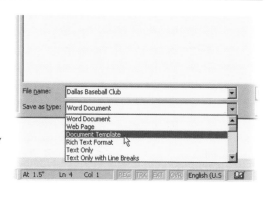

● Click on the down arrow
next to the **Save as type:**
text box and select
Document Template
(*.dot**).

● Now the file type has
changed to a template file.
Click on **Save**.

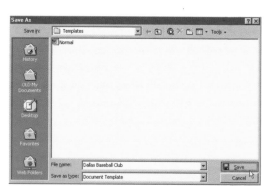

● Close the new template
file by selecting **Close** from
the **File** menu.

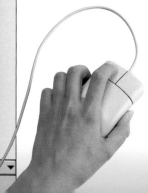

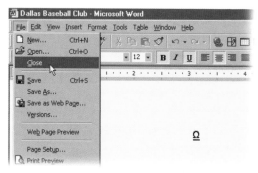

42 **Opening the
normal template**

USING THE NEW TEMPLATE

The more that you use a template that you have created, the sooner you will discover how useful and time-saving they are. And now that you have found out how easy they are to create, don't be surprised if eventually you find yourself creating more templates and using them more often than the default templates provided by Word.

USING THE NEW TEMPLATE

● To write an agenda using the new template, begin by clicking on **New...** in the **File** menu.

● The **New** dialog box opens. Click on the **General** tab at the top if its contents are not visible.

● You will see the **Dallas Baseball Club** template in the window. Click on the template and click on **OK**.

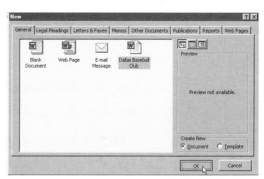

● A new document opens containing the text and formatting that was entered into the **Dallas Baseball Club** template. You can now write a new agenda and save it as a document with its own file name. The original template remains intact and ready for you to use again.

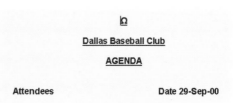

DOCUMENT SHORTCUTS

**Word has many time-saving ways of dealing with documents.
You can view different parts of a document simultaneously,
merge documents, and use Undo, Redo, and Find and Replace.**

VIEWING, MERGING, AND FINDING

Formatting a document and entering the text are central to word processing. However, Word contains many features that make it easy to deal with documents. These include methods of viewing one or more documents.

1 SPLITTING THE SCREEN

● When working with long documents, it can be useful to split the document onscreen to view different parts of it at the same time. This reduces having to scroll down the document.

● With the document open, position the cursor over the split box at the top of the vertical scroll bar. The cursor changes into two short horizontal bars with a vertical two-way arrow, sometimes called the split-screen cursor.

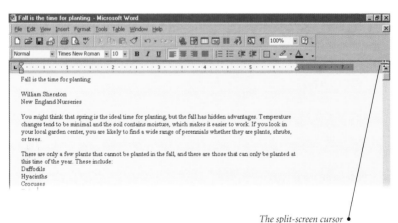

The split-screen cursor ●

● Hold down the left mouse button and drag the split-screen cursor downward. A horizontal line appears across the screen showing where the split will occur.

● Release the mouse button and the document is displayed in two panes, which you can click on, scroll through, and make changes to the document.

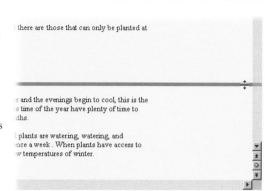

2 MULTIPLE DOCUMENTS

● If you are working on related documents, it can be useful to view them onscreen simultaneously.

● Open the two documents that you wish to view, click on **Windows** on the Menu bar and select **Arrange All**.

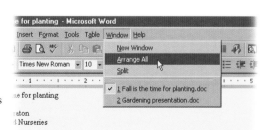

● Two half-screens appear. To edit either document, click in the half-screen and continue with the word processing as usual. The title bar at the top of the half-screen is blue when it is the active window.

● To revert to a single window again, click on the Maximize or Restore button of the document that you wish to see in full.

The active half-screen ●

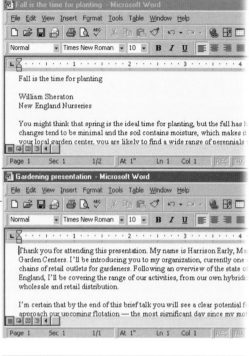

3 MERGING DOCUMENTS

● If you have written several documents that you wish to merge, you can do this by using **Insert**.

● Open the main document and place the insertion point where the second file is to be inserted. Click on **Insert** on the Menu bar and select **File...** .

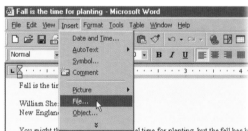

● The **Insert File** dialog box appears. You can use the **Look in:** box to navigate to the location of the file that you want to insert. Click on the document's file name and click on **Insert** at the foot of the window.

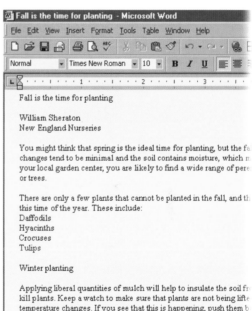

● The file is now merged with the main document. You can use the **Insert** command to merge as many documents into one as you need.

Fall is the time for planting

William Sheraton
New England Nurseries

You might think that spring is the ideal time for planting, but the fa
changes tend to be minimal and the soil contains moisture, which n
your local garden center, you are likely to find a wide range of pere
or trees.

There are only a few plants that cannot be planted in the fall, and th
this time of the year. These include:
Daffodils
Hyacinths
Crocuses
Tulips

Winter planting

Applying liberal quantities of mulch will help to insulate the soil fr
kill plants. Keep a watch to make sure that plants are not being lift
temperature changes. If you see that this is happening, push them b
roots from being exposed.

With peonies, it is essential that they be planted so the eyes (growi
2 inches below the soil surface. If planted too deep, they will not bl
enough, the eyes may be damaged by winter cold.

Removing the split screen

To revert to only having one document window after you have split the screen, position the cursor over the split bar until it turns into the two-way arrow, then double-click on the left mouse button.

4 UNDO & REDO COMMANDS

● As you type in or move text, Word maintains a record of your actions, which you can undo, and then redo if necessary, by using the **Undo** and **Redo** buttons on the Standard toolbar.

● To see how they work, open a new document and type in: **A demonstration of the Undo and Redo commands.** Use the Tab⇆ key to move the text to the right-hand side of the page.

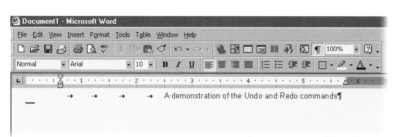

● Click on the **Undo** button on the Standard toolbar.
● The highlighted text is moved back to the left by one tab position.

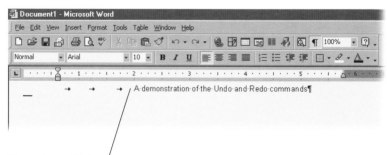

The text is moved back to the left by one tab position

● Continue clicking on the **Undo** button until you have undone all actions. This includes the sample sentence that you typed in, which will be removed from the document.

● The actions that were first carried out can now be redone by using the **Redo** button. Click on the **Redo** button next to the **Undo** button. For each click you will see the text and tab positions reinstated.

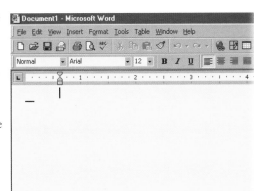

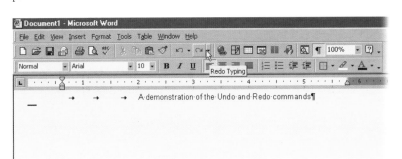

THE UNDO MENU

Word keeps an extensive list of the actions that you can undo and redo. To see the lists of actions, click on the down arrow next to the **Undo** and **Redo** buttons. From the drop-down menu you can select, for example, the last six actions to undo. Don't worry if you make a mistake – you can always redo them again. The drop-down menu displays six actions at a time. To see the previous actions, you can use the scroll bar to the right.

5 FIND AND REPLACE

● When creating documents, you may discover that you have misspelled a word or name throughout the document, or you may wish to use a different word, such as **disc** instead of **disk**. Using the **Find and Replace** command, you only need enter the word to find, and enter the replacement word, and Word replaces the error when you instruct Word to do so.

● An outline timetable for a two-day sales executives' training course might contain entries as shown in the example at right.

● Due to circumstances beyond the organizers' control, the first day of the course has to be brought forward by one day. Select **Replace...** from the **Edit** menu.

● The **Find and Replace** dialog box opens. Enter **Tuesday** in the **Find what:** box, enter **Monday** in the **Replace with:** box, and click on **Replace All**.

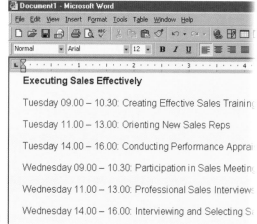

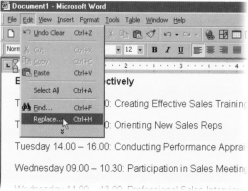

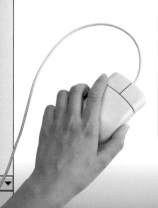

● A message is displayed that three replacements have been made. Click on **OK**.

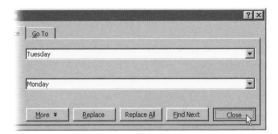

● Click on **Close** at the foot of the dialog box.

● The timetable now shows the course taking place on Monday and Wednesday.
● By using the **Replace...** button rather than **Replace All**, you can replace each instance of a word for another, one at a time. This is useful if you do not need to replace all occurrences of a word. If you use the **Find Next** button, Word highlights each occurrence of the word without replacing it. If you then decide to replace it, click on the **Replace...** button.

Executing Sales Effectively

Monday 09.00 – 10.30: Creating Effective Sales Training

Monday 11.00 – 13.00: Orienting New Sales Reps

Monday 14.00 – 16.00: Conducting Performance Apprai

Wednesday 09.00 – 10.30: Participation in Sales Meetin

Wednesday 11.00 – 13.00: Professional Sales Interviews

Wednesday 14.00 – 16.00: Interviewing and Selecting Sa

FINDING WITHOUT REPLACING

If you need to find a word in your document without replacing it, click on **Edit** on the Menu bar and then on **Find**. With a click on the **Find Next** button, the next instance of the word is displayed and highlighted. At the end of the document, a message box will appear, offering options or stating that the search is finished. To cancel a word search while it is in progress, press the [Esc] key.

KEYBOARD SHORTCUTS

In Microsoft Word 2000, a large number of tasks can be achieved using keyboard shortcuts. A basic knowledge of these can save you time and effort when producing a document.

USING THE KEYS

This section of the book provides lists of the most commonly used keyboard shortcuts. The section begins by showing how it's possible to work through a piece of unformatted text and apply formats and styles using only keyboard shortcuts. Many of these involve using letter keys together with Ctrl, Alt, and ⇧ Shift.

Key combinations
When two keys are used, one is held down while the other is pressed. For example, the shortcut Ctrl + **O** means hold down Ctrl and press **O** (to open a document). More complex commands use three keys, two of which are held down while the third is pressed. For example, to change to small capitals, use Ctrl + ⇧ Shift + **K**, meaning hold down Ctrl and ⇧ Shift, and then press **K**. The text must first be highlighted.

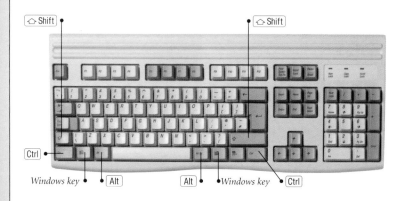

OPENING A NEW DOCUMENT

● C + N

Pressing these two keys opens a new blank document.

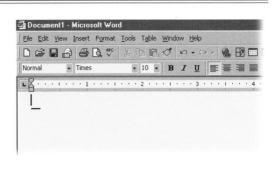

● The illustration on the right shows the basic document that will be used to show how and when keyboard shortcuts are used. If you wish to work through the example, key in the text on which to work.

SELECTING ALL

● [Ctrl] + A

This combination selects all the text in the document so that you can, for example, change the font for the whole document.

All the text in the ●
document is selected

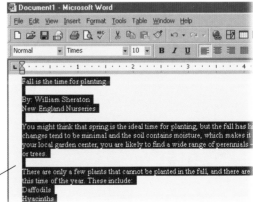

SELECTING TEXT TO THE END OF A LINE

● ⇧Shift + End

Place the cursor at the beginning of the text. Press these keys to highlight the text to the end of the line.

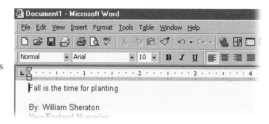

The text is highlighted to the end of the line ●

CENTERING THE TEXT

● Ctrl + E

With the text selected, press these keys to center the text.

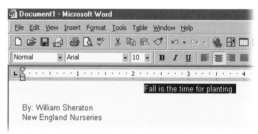

CHANGING THE FONT SIZE

● Ctrl + ⇧ Shift + >
The font size of any highlighted text can be increased by using these keys. Each press of the combination increases the font size by one point.

● To reduce the font size, press Ctrl + ⇧ Shift + <

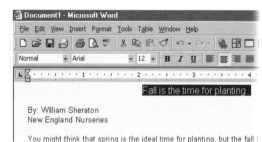

DOUBLE UNDERLINING TEXT

● Ctrl + ⇧ Shift + D
Any highlighted text can be double underlined with these keys.

The text is double underlined ●

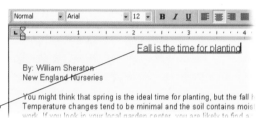

INDENTING TEXT

● Ctrl + M
Highlighted text can be indented using these keys. Press the combination once for each half-inch indent.

The text is indented ●

● To decrease the indent in half-inch steps, press Ctrl + ⇧ Shift + M.

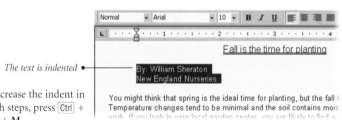

SELECTING A WORD AT A TIME

● Ctrl + ⇧ Shift + →

This combination selects one word to the right of the cursor.

Place the cursor at the beginning of the word ●

One word to the right of the cursor is selected ●

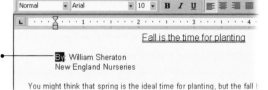

MAKING TEXT ITALIC

● Ctrl + I

Pressing these keys italicizes the highlighted text.

The italicized text ●

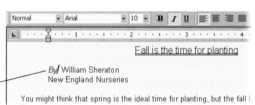

MAKING TEXT BOLD

● Ctrl + B

This combination of keys emboldens the highlighted text.

Emboldened text ●

CHANGING TO SMALL CAPITALS

● Ctrl + ⇧ Shift + **K**

This key combination changes the highlighted text to an initial capital followed by small capitals.

Small caps •

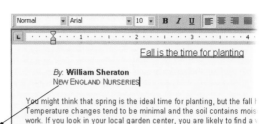

JUSTIFYING A PARAGRAPH

● Ctrl + **J**

To make both ends of the lines of a paragraph align vertically, (called *justified* text), highlight the paragraph and use this combination of keys.

Justified text •

OPERATIONS ON THE DOCUMENT

SAVING A DOCUMENT

● Ctrl + **S**

This combination of keys is one of the most useful for saving your work both while it is in progress and when you have finished.

PRINTING A DOCUMENT

● Ctrl + **P**

This key combination opens the **Print** dialog box where you are prompted to answer questions in preparation for printing.

CLOSING A DOCUMENT

● Ctrl + **W**

Pressing these keys closes the active document. If the document has not been saved, you will be prompted to save it.

SHORTCUT GLOSSARY

There are something in the region of 300 keyboard shortcuts available in Word 2000. This chapter consists of a glossary of the most useful and commonly used shortcuts.

LEARNING SHORTCUTS

Learning shortcuts is probably the most avoided activity in word processing. Everyone acknowledges their usefulness, but at any particular point it seems easier and faster to use the the menu options, for example, rather than spend a few seconds to learn and remember key combinations that will eventually save you a lot of time. Here a selection is presented to help you begin to learn Word's shortcuts.

WORKING WITH DOCUMENTS

A range of keyboard shortcuts allows you to carry out operations that affect the whole of the document. Several of these will open a dialog box.

For example, [Ctrl] + O (to open a document) will bring up a dialog box prompting you to choose the Word document that you want to open.

*Pressing the F12 key, (above), has the effect of opening the **Save As** dialog box.*

To Open a document . . . . [Ctrl] + O
To Save a document . . . . [Ctrl] + S
To Save a document as
(giving the document a
new name) F12
To Close a document . . . . [Ctrl] + W
To Print a document . . . . [Ctrl] + P
To Create a new
document in the same
style as the most recent . . . . [Ctrl] + N
To View document as
Print Layout . . . .[Ctrl] + [Alt] + P
To View document as
Normal . . . . [Ctrl] + [Alt] + N

POSITIONING THE INSERTION POINT IN THE TEXT AND THE DOCUMENT

These shortcuts enable you to move the insertion point on a page or between pages without using the mouse. Many require the use of the keyboard cursor arrows and of the Page Up `PgUp`, Page Down `PgDn`, and Home `Home` keys.

To Move the Insertion point:

One character to the left	`←`
One character to the right	`→`
One word to the left	`Ctrl` + `←`
One word to the right	`Ctrl` + `→`
One paragraph up	`Ctrl` + `↑`
One paragraph down	`Ctrl` + `↓`
One line up	`↑`
One line down	`↓`
To the end of the current line of text	`End`
To the beginning of the current line of text	`Home`
To the top of the current document window	`Ctrl` + `Alt` + `PgUp`
To the bottom of the current document window	`Ctrl` + `Alt` + `PgDn`
Up one screen (scrolling through document)	`PgUp`
Down one screen (scrolling through document)	`PgDn`
To the top of the next document page	`Ctrl` + `PgDn`
To the top of the previous document page	`Ctrl` + `PgUp`
To the end of the document	`Ctrl` + `End`
To the beginning of the document	`Ctrl` + `Home`

Used in combination with the `Ctrl` *key, the keyboard cursor keys will move the insertion point back and forth along a line a word at a time, or up and down the page a paragraph at a time.*

SELECTING TEXT

Select one character to the right	Shift + →
Select one character to the left	Shift + ←
Select one word to the right	Ctrl, Shift + →
Select one word to the left	Ctrl, Shift + ←
Select text to end of line	Shift + End
Select text to beginning of line	Shift + Home
Select text of current line and then each line downward	Shift + ↓
Select text of current line and then each line upward	Shift + ↑
Select text to the end of the current paragraph	Ctrl + Shift + ↓
Select text to the beginning of the current paragraph	Ctrl + Shift + ↑
Select text to the beginning of the document	Ctrl + Shift + Home
Select text to the end of the document	Ctrl + Shift + End
Undo an action	Ctrl + Z
Redo an action	Ctrl + Y

DELETING TEXT

There is a difference between deleting text and cutting it, in that deleted text cannot be pasted back onto the page (see Copying and Pasting Text opposite).

Delete one character to the left	← Bksp
Delete one word to the left	Ctrl + ← Bksp
Delete one character to the right	Del
Delete one word to the right	Ctrl + Del
Cut selected text to the Clipboard	Ctrl + X

The illustration shows the key combination to delete one word to the right of the cursor position: Ctrl + Del.

COPYING AND PASTING TEXT

These two keyboard shortcuts are probably the most widely used of all. They can be used not only in Word but in most Microsoft® programs and many others, too.

Copy selected text to the Clipboard . . . . Ctrl + C
Paste copied text into a document . . . . Ctrl + V

Copying and pasting using the keyboard can save a great deal of time once you are used to this easy option.

EDITING TEXT

The editing keyboard shortcuts will only apply to text that has been highlighted. Select your text using the shortcuts outlined above or by using the mouse if it is more convenient. Note that these shortcuts are "toggles" – that is they "switch" on and off the editing functions. Thus, for example, to make text bold select the text, hold down the Ctrl key and press the letter **B** key. To revert to normal text, you use the same Ctrl and letter **B** keys.

Make text bold . . . . Ctrl + B
Make text italics . . . . Ctrl + I
Make text underlined . . . . Ctrl + U
Make words only underlined . . . . Ctrl + Shift + W
Make text double underlined . . . . Ctrl + Shift + D
Make text all capital letters . . . . Ctrl + Shift + A
Allow changes to the font style . . . . Ctrl + Shift + F
Allow changes to the font size . . . . Ctrl + Shift + P
Increase font size . . . . Ctrl + Shift + >
Decrease font size . . . . Ctrl + Shift + <
Format the text as small capital letters . . . . Ctrl + Shift + K

The font size of any selected text can be quickly decreased by using the key combination: Ctrl + Shift + <

SETTING UP LINE SPACING IN A DOCUMENT

Select the text in which you wish to alter the line spacing and press the keys detailed below. These keys are not toggle keys and if, for example, you have altered the line spacing for some text to be double and then wish the spacing to be single again, you have to reselect the text and enter Ctrl and 1.

Make text single line spacing.............................. Ctrl + 1
Make text double line spacing.............................. Ctrl + 2
Make text 1.5 line spacing................................. Ctrl + 5

INSERTING BREAKS IN A DOCUMENT

To insert a break in a document, position the insertion point where you want the page break or line break and then press the appropriate keys.

Insert a page break............. Ctrl + Enter ←⤶
Insert a line break.............. Enter ←⤶

You can determine yourself where a page ends by placing the cursor at that point and pressing Ctrl + Enter ←⤶.

ALIGNING PARAGRAPHS IN A DOCUMENT

To change the alignment of a paragraph (which may be just a single line), select the paragraphs you wish to align and then enter the keys detailed below.

Centre a paragraph .... Ctrl + E
Right align a paragraph................................ Ctrl + R
Justify a paragraph................................... Ctrl + J
Left align a paragraph .... Ctrl + L
Indent a paragraph on the left .... Ctrl + M
Remove an indent from a paragraph
on the left.. Ctrl + Shift + M
Create a hanging indent .... Ctrl + T
Reduce a hanging indent.............................. Ctrl + Shift + T
Remove paragraph formatting .... Ctrl + Q

WORKING WITH DOCUMENT WINDOWS

Some newer keyboards now incorporate a Windows key that displays the Start Menu.

The Function keys (or F keys as they are also known) used in the following sections are shown as F1 through to F12. The keys can be found in the top row above the main part of the keyboard area.

Display the Clipboard . . . . `Ctrl` + C; `Ctrl` + C
Maximize the document window . . . . `Ctrl` + F10
Minimize the document window . . . . `Ctrl` + F5
Split the document window . . . . `Ctrl` + `Alt` + W
Close the document window . . . . `Ctrl` + W
Quit the Word program . . . . `Alt` + F4
Display the Start menu . . . . Windows key

WORKING WITH MENUS VIA THE FUNCTION KEYS

Some of the actions available in the drop-down menus are also available via the function keys at the top of the keyboard. As well as simple operations such as **Save As** (carried out by pressing F12), these actions also include several of the more complex functions in Word, such as checking Spelling and Grammar, getting Microsoft Office Assistant Help, and opening the Thesaurus.

Microsoft Office Assistant Help F1
Print Preview. . . . . `Ctrl` + F2
Find and Replace dialog box. F5
Spelling and Grammar dialog box F7
Thesaurus . . . . `Shift` + F7

To see on screen how the printed version of your document will appear, hold down the `Ctrl` key and press F2 to change to Print Preview.

GLOSSARY

ALIGNMENT
In word processing, this refers to the side of the text that is aligned in a straight vertical line along one side (for example, left-aligned text is straight on the left side, and the ends of the lines are ragged on the right).

AUTOCORRECT
A feature of Word that can be used either to correct errors that you make frequently, or to translate a few keystrokes into text that you have previously defined.

AUTOTEXT
Word's AutoText feature provides the facility to specify text and its related formatting, which Word inserts when you enter a sequence of characters that you have previously linked to the specified text.

BUTTONS
These are another name for the individual icons on the toolbar, for example, the print button on the Standard toolbar, which contains an icon of a printer

CENTERED TEXT
One or more lines of text that are laid out on the page centered around the midpoint of the text area of a document.

COPY
To copy part of the text so that the same piece of text can be "pasted" into a new position (in the same document or another document) without removing the original piece of text.

CUSTOM DICTIONARY
A dictionary separate from the main dictionary, which can contain spellings defined by the user. It is possible to have more than one custom dictionary for different kinds of text, such as scientific or mathematical.

CUT
To remove a block of text, either to delete it permanently or to "paste" it into a new position in the same document or another document.

DEFAULT SETTINGS
These are settings that may include, for example, layouts, formats, or fonts that Word is programmed to use unless instructed to do otherwise by the user.

DIALOG BOX
This is a special window displayed on the screen that contains a set of options for the user to choose from. After the choices have been made, the user usually clicks on OK, Close, or Cancel to return to the document.

FUNCTION KEYS
These are the keys labelled F1, F2, F3 and so on, usually placed along the top of the keyboard. They are used to provide shortcuts to common instructions or to a feature that is not otherwise available.

INDENT
Indenting shifts part of the text, or just the first line in every paragraph, across the screen.

INSERTION POINT
A blinking upright line on the screen. As you type, text appears at the insertion point.

JUSTIFIED TEXT
Text that is aligned on both left and right sides, so there is no ragged edge either side.

MARGIN
The distance between the text and the paper edge. There are four margins on a page: top, bottom, left, and right.

RADIO BUTTON
A small circle next to an option in a dialog box, which is either empty or contains a small black circle indicating that the option has been selected. Named for the knobs on early radio sets.

SCROLL BARS
Bars at the foot and the right of the screen that can be used to move through the document. The vertical bar (on the right) is the more useful.

TABS
Preset or customized positions along one or more lines of text. Text will be aligned down the page against these positions when the tab position is reached after pressing the tab key.

TEMPLATE
A special document that can contain formats, styles, and layouts, as well as customized text and graphics. Any new document that is opened and based on a specific template will contain all the text, graphics, and settings in the template.

INDEX

ACKNOWLEDGMENTS

PUBLISHER'S ACKNOWLEDGMENTS
Dorling Kindersley would like to thank the following:
Paul Mattock of APM, Brighton, for commissioned photography.
Microsoft Corporation for permission to reproduce screens
from within Microsoft® Word 2000.

Every effort has been made to trace the copyright holders.
The publisher apologizes for any unintentional omissions and would be pleased,
in such cases, to place an acknowledgment in future editions of this book.

Microsoft® is a registered trademark of Microsoft Corporation
in the United States and/or other countries.